Pregnant With Cancer

First Published in Great Britain in 2011
By Lulu.com

ISBN Number: 978-1-4477-2263-2

Cover designed by: James Beach Design, UK

www.cancercoachuk.com

Lulu.com

I dedicate this book to my selfless and loving Mum; my patient and long suffering partner, Laith; my amazing daughter and inspiration, Laila, and the star of this book, Ruby, who started this journey with me.

You have allowed me the space to get through my treatment and recover from the whirlwind that descends with a cancer diagnosis.

Thank you.

I owe you all my life.

Foreword

I met Daniella Slabbert when she invited me to edit the account of her journey through the diagnosis and treatment of her breast cancer, which coincided with her longed-for second pregnancy.

Her story is one of unending hope and courage. I was moved to tears by her determination and strength of spirit, and I feel privileged to have made a very small contribution to the telling of her story.

I am proud to know Daniella and her incredibly supportive network of family, friends and health professionals. I wish them all good health and happiness.

Sheila Grimes
Torrance, CA
May, 2011

Pregnant with Cancer: A Woman's Journey

In 2007 I was diagnosed with breast cancer and that diagnosis started me on a journey of self-discovery that has taken me to the depths of hell and to the highest mountain tops. One of the ways I tried to deal with the ordeal of cancer was to write about my experiences. This account has been adapted from my blog.

As time has passed since my treatment ended and the last of the chains that hold me to cancer start to fade, I am adamant about sharing my story and even if it inspires only one person, it will have been worth it.

I have also learned a great many things since my diagnosis and these are things that have carried me through many really tough times. I want to share these resources with people embarking on this journey.

Thank you for taking the time to read this and I really hope you find some solace in the following pages.

Daniella Slabbert
London
May 2009

Table of Contents

My Diagnosis   Page 1

Life Without The Lump   Page 8

My First Poison   Page 10

Trying To Figure It All Out   Page 12

The Sun Is Shining And My Spirits Are Lifted   Page 14

A Second Sip From The Poisoned Chalice   Page 16

What A Difference A Day Makes   Page 19

A Stitch In Time...   Page 23

Let Nature Take Its Course   Page 28

And Life Takes Over   Page 32

Taking A Stand   Page 36

The Big Move   Page 37

Closer to Home   Page 38

The Poison Is Flowing Again   Page 39

A New Hair Day   Page 41

Sunday Night Reflections   Page 43

Counting Blessings   Page 45

Table of Contents, continued

And The Poison Kicks In   Page 47

Good Old Garlic   Page 49

Thoughts For The Day   Page 51

Spirits Are Lifting   Page 55

It's Sunday Night Again And I'm Reflecting   Page 56

It's Been Three Weeks Already…   Page 58
And Another Cup Of Poison

Home At Last   Page 61

A Name For A Little Princess   Page 63

Out With The Old And In With The New   Page 65
(Even If It Is Fake)

Birthday Blues   Page 67

Party Time   Page 69

The Poison With A Sting In Its Tail…   Page 71

Time Passes So Quickly   Page 73

Reality Really Bites   Page 75

What A Day…   Page 78

How I Would Love To Get Off This Ride   Page 80

Table of Contents, continued

Ruby   Page 82

Getting It Together   Page 84

The Poison Chalice Revisited   Page 85

Mum's The Word   Page 87

Time Out   Page 90

Out On A Limb   Page 94

It's Been A Long Day   Page 97

Happy Birthday Little Angel!   Page 98

The Beginning Of The End   Page 99

Let's Run With It...   Page 101

At Long Last   Page 102

Moving On...   Page 105

No Time For Regret   Page 107

Visiting An Old Haunt...   Page 110

Afterword   Page 111

March 3rd 2007
My Diagnosis

2007... It was supposed to be a quiet year with us settling into a geared down pace of life. We moved into our first proper family home in July 2006. My partner, Laith, had a good job and I concentrated on being a Mum and homemaker, arranging birthday parties for my family and, for the first time in a long time, just enjoying life.

I had had 2 miscarriages (one in January 2006 and one in June 2006) but we were still determined about getting pregnant again ASAP as our daughter had just turned 2 and we wanted a sibling for her. Our ideal number of children would be three.

After our daughter's birthday in September, I was watching the Sharon Osborne show and they had a cancer awareness programme on. That night I was having a bath and made a point of checking my breasts. I felt a small lump on the left near the armpit. The next morning I called my surgery and got an appointment to get it checked out. The doctor seemed convinced it was nothing to worry about and told me to come back in three weeks to check it again at a different time in my 'cycle'. I did this and it was still there. He was still convinced it was nothing but I insisted that I wanted it checked out.

My first breast clinic appointment was six weeks later. Yes, **six** weeks. During those six weeks we realised I was pregnant. I went to the breast appointment with other priorities on my mind. They did a mammogram (using a very heavy lead apron as I was pregnant) and did a scan as well as a biopsy (which was excruciatingly painful). I had an appointment a week later for the results. During the week the hospital called and said that the doctors wanted to do a mammogram on the other breast just as a precaution. This should have rung alarm bells with me but it was more of an inconvenience, and I wasn't concerned. I just wanted to get on with the business of being pregnant.

As for the pregnancy, it was detected during a routine scan that both of the baby's feet were clubbed, which in itself is not a big deal except that it could be an indicator of a chromosomal abnormality (Down syndrome, etc.). I also needed to have my cervix stitched closed as a precaution after my two previous miscarriages where my womb had opened early (at 22 weeks).

So, my week schedule ran as follows... Wednesday: surgical sutures (stitches to cervix) and Thursday the biopsy results. The surgery was delayed by a day as the hospital was overbooked on surgeries so the biopsy results were delayed until the following week.

I went in to see the consultant the next week. They spent ages doing another mammogram and scanning my right breast. I was then taken in to the consultant's office and told that the biopsy on the lump was 'malignant' and that they wanted to do a biopsy on the other breast the next day. They did not use the words cancer but eventually it dawned on me. They spoke of chemotherapy and that it was safe to do while pregnant; but none of it really hit home. I was sort of in a world of my own while all else around me was like a distant movie. I drove myself home in tears, still struggling to comprehend what had just happened. What did this all mean?

The second biopsy was benign (no cancer) and the consultant and breast nurse were very open and forthcoming about my options and very positive about it all being quite routine and the ordeal being over by the end of the year.

That was just the beginning of the roller coaster ride that was to follow.

This was very much the start of my journey. Finding the will to be positive about my pregnancy as well as finding out about cancer; the survival rates, the alternative treatments and just generally doing too much research and scaring myself. It was also a time of trying to get my daughter into nursery as soon as possible and re-organizing our lives. It was a trying time to say the least.

On reflection: Even if you are low risk and young and healthy, check yourself for lumps once a month at least. Get to know what your breasts feel like and notice any differences.

Get to the doctor as soon as possible if you find a change; and don't be 'dismissed'. Make sure you get it properly checked out even if you have to challenge your GP. They don't know everything and aren't always right.

The Beginning Of The Ride
(added as a note)

I remember going into hospital for the lumpectomy. They had the obstetrician (baby delivery doctor) on hand in case I lost the pregnancy. The anaesthetist's only words to me, as I was being wheeled into theatre were, 'Don't expect the baby to still be there when you wake up.' Which I thought was a little insensitive; but the baby was determined and hung in there all through the operation. I awoke to find myself in the gynaecological ward with a bag and tubes draining the blood and fluid from my wound; and baby still in situ.

I also had a text from my father to say that my grandmother had passed away and that he had just come from her funeral. My father lives in South Africa and we don't connect nearly often enough. My grandmother and I had been writing to each other for years but I regret that she never got to meet her first great-grandchildren. I then sent him a text back that I had just had an operation and I have cancer. I don't think that he had a very good day that day.

On reflection: Professionals do not always know everything and cannot account for the human spirit. The human spirit can defy medical opinion if you let it.

March 29th 2007
Life Without The Lump

So the malignant lump was removed in March, as well as lymph nodes under my arm. I found myself at home in pain and not being able to take much for the pain other than paracetamol because of the pregnancy. My mobility was severely limited and the pain was excruciating. I had a hard time driving the car and changing gears.

I had a few really down days where I would break down into floods of tears for no apparent reason but generally speaking, we just carried on with life as normal. I found that I became tired very easily but Laith, my partner and father of my children was fantastic and gave me loads of space to rest and sleep as and when I needed it.

I occasionally found that morbid thoughts would come into my head; like what needed to be organized before I died, or getting really sentimental about my legacy to the world. But the most devastating and most motivating thought was of another woman bringing up my daughter. That really got to me; a stepmother who would never be able to love my daughter as much as I do and who would instil in her morals and belief systems different to mine and which I may not agree with. This, more than anything else, motivated me to keep positive and to **LIVE** so I can be there for her for as long as possible.

The lesson here is to find something powerful to motivate you through the tough times. Something to live for.

Just a few days later...
March 31st 2007
My First Poison

I had my first dose of chemotherapy yesterday. I'm not sure what I was expecting but I feel pretty normal. I guess I expected it to hurt and I think I expected to feel rotten. I'm sure it will kick in at some point, but right now I feel like I should get through this OK.

I am naturally very aware of any slight reactions I may be experiencing as I have a little guest to consider.

We also had an antenatal appointment yesterday and baby is fine. He's kicking away and very responsive to prodding. Although I know I am in good hands with my oncologist and I know he has treated pregnant women before, I still worry about what effect the chemotherapy will have on the poor little thing. He is either going to be born a Mummy's child or he will have huge issues with me for putting him through this trauma at a time when I should be nurturing him. Oh, by the way, we don't know if it's a boy or a girl but I keep calling it 'him'.

The lesson I take away from this is: Don't expect the worst. It's not always that bad. Chemotherapy has different side effects with different people. Just don't expect the worst.

April 4th 2007
Trying To Figure It All Out

I'm in my 27th week of pregnancy now and have started getting a bit of heartburn (for the first time). Baby is fairly quiet and has been since the chemo but as long as I feel him moving occasionally, I won't worry.

My arm is getting stronger all the time and feeling is coming back to the nerves. The pain is not as sharp and I have not had any pain pills since the chemo last week.

I have had a few days of being completely exhausted but hopefully, once the sun is out, my spirits will pick up and my energy levels will shoot up.

No hair has fallen out yet but I have an appointment to choose a wig on the 12th. It's all very strange but am almost looking forward to not having to worry about washing or dyeing my hair for a while; also not having to shave will be a small bonus.

Note to self: Every cloud has a silver lining. Find yours, no matter how small and insignificant.

April 8th 2007
The Sun Is Shining And My Spirits Are Lifted

It's a beautiful Sunday here in London. The sun is shining and it's warm. I'm oddly energetic. My arm is so much better and almost back to normal. It's been amazing.

This brings me on to a subject I have been thinking a lot about. Why the hell am I sick? There is no history of any kind of cancer in my family and I am a fairly healthy eater. I am wary of chemicals in my environment and won't use any harsh cleaning products, etc.

I was reading a book (*Anatomy of the Spirit* by Caroline Myss, PhD), which suggests that our physical conditions are a result of our emotional states and that sickness demonstrates a lack of power in certain areas of our lives.

The more I think about this, the more sense it makes to me and the more I can relate to its truth. Over the past two years or so I have been aware of a distinct lack of power in certain areas of my life. I need to address these areas if I am to heal and stay healthy. It's that elusive balance, which is so very important in the grand scheme of things.

The process starts here and now and I will take control. By relinquishing ultimate control to the powers that be, I will be able to free up my own resources to heal and work on those areas that need attention so desperately. I hereby begin my journey.

It is so important to be aware of your emotions and know that you are experiencing emotional pain for a reason. It's there to tell you to pay attention; and if you don't listen, it may develop into something more.

April 21st 2007
A Second Sip From The Poisoned Chalice

We decided on the spur of the moment to make a run for it and head off to France for some down time. It was a two day drive down and two days back, but worth it. I must admit, I was a little nervous about being too far away from the hospital and the doctors treating me.

All was fine until the morning we left to come back to London. I woke up with a really sore arm and feeling somewhat under the weather. By the time we left, I was practically in tears and feeling awful. We drove back via Mont Blanc (the highest peak of the Alps). I slept most of the first day but Mont Blanc lifted my spirits. What an awesome place.

After a good night's sleep and another day on the road, we finally arrived home. I still felt off-colour and my arm was useless. I had an appointment at the hospital for blood tests on the following morning. I mentioned how I was feeling and the doctor prescribed some antibiotics for me in case of infection. He was a little less impressed with me going abroad without telling anyone after my first chemo.

So Thursday arrived and my second chemo treatment. The needle went in without any bruising (and on the first attempt) and the drugs just filtered into my system. As yet I have had no side effects to speak of. Even my hair seems to be holding its own for the time being.

Baby is growing and very active. He gets a bit quiet after chemo for a few days. Apparently the chemo drugs do not significantly cross the placenta, so he is protected from the effects of the chemo (which is very good news).

I still have loads of questions, like: what are the chances of the baby having cancer? I know he won't have breast cancer as you have to be an adolescent before that becomes a possibility, but perhaps there was a cancer cell roaming around at conception. All will become clear when baby decides to make his appearance.

April 30th 2007
What A Difference A Day Makes

So this morning I got up, just like any other morning and went through the motions of getting myself and my daughter Laila ready for the day (with a lot of help from my partner, Laith). We all bundled into the car at about 8 am and dropped Laith off to catch a train for work and I then took Laila to nursery for her first full day. A bog standard morning by all accounts.

I got home and felt a bit tired so took it easy for a while. I went upstairs for a bath and while running the water I felt what I thought to be a large amount of discharge soaking my knickers. On checking, it seemed more watery than a standard discharge, which niggled me a little. After my bath I plucked up the courage to call my GP who advised me to call the midwives, which I did. They asked me to come in.

After assessment they confirmed my fear; my membrane had ruptured and it was amniotic fluid that had been discharged. There was no sign of infection and I hadn't gone into labour (which is good news by all accounts).

Anyway, I am now being monitored in hospital and will be here for at least ten days to check for infection to either myself or baby. They will be taking the sutures out tomorrow, which means the neck of my womb may start to open (dilate). With the help of a good friend's Mum, (www.hartlands.co.uk) who often works with babies remotely using energetic healing, I am confident all is well. I am on antibiotics, and baby, through a huge injection in my derriere, is getting steroids to develop his lungs in case I go into labour and we have to deliver him. He's a strong little thing, having stuck with me through all the crap we have had to deal with.

There are so many amazing people that also need thanking, the staff at the Homerton in, London, for their completely professional and fantastic personal support and in whose hands I completely trust the welfare of my baby and myself. Also my oncologist and his brilliant team from the Queen Elizabeth hospital, who answers questions no matter how difficult it may be to hear what he has to say and who I also trust completely with my life as well as that of my unborn child.

Also my friends and family who have been there with practical and spiritual support from the word go. Your presence in my life has been unconditional and beyond the call of friendship and I have no words to tell you how truly grateful I am for all your love and support and generosity, and what a difference it has made to me.

And then, of course, I need to let Laith know that he has been the one person without whose support I would have given up ages ago. He has been my backbone through all of this and keeps me strong and has been the best friend and partner I could dream of. The one person I can be a wreck with and who I can be totally honest with, and I know he will be able to pull me out of the doldrums and support me in any way, shape or form. I love you. And then of course there is Laila, who I miss so much while in hospital and who keeps me sane and focused and intent on getting through this in one piece; emotionally, physically and spiritually. It's all for you, baby girl.

My lesson for the day is: Don't underestimate or take for granted the network of people around you.

April 30th 2007
A Stitch In Time...

It's so strange. Laith and I were chatting last night about how amazing life is, and how forces beyond our control will orchestrate our situations and environment to best suit our needs; and we are blissfully unaware of any of it until things happen in our lives and we realize that actually we are in the best place for this to have happened and that we had no idea or control over it.

A bit like fate, well it *is* fate really, although fatalism is often talked about as a dirty word or concept. I won't bore you with all the examples I can think of but our life situation is optimal for being able to deal with and cope with all that has happened to us. We are surrounded by a fantastic network of friends who live in very close proximity and who all have little ones of their own and are fantastically supportive. Then there is the local hospital where my oncologist has had experience of dealing with pregnant ladies needing chemo. This is a rare situation according to everyone I have spoken to, so it's 'fate' that has brought me under his wing.

On a smaller scale, we went off to France last week completely confident that no emergencies would befall us. I felt great and was completely comfortable and confident about the pregnancy. The trip was long, and the van is not as comfortable as a car might have been, and I was more physically active in France than I would normally be back home. As I mentioned before, we got home in one piece and all was fine, then this week, exactly a week after getting back, my waters go and I need an op to remove my suture. It's like fate kept me safe while away from home but as soon as we had arrived home and settled in; my chemo was out of the way and Laila was inducted into nursery (literally on her first full day at nursery) my body allows itself to just let go. There are a number of other things involving finance and work but I won't go into that. It's just all so perfectly worked out, and not by me.

With reference to the heading of this entry, my stitches were taken out this morning in all of five minutes. Gas and air helped me cope with the discomfort but all are out and I am resting up in the ward. I was a bit flushed this morning but I think that is a side effect of the chemo, as it also happened after the first treatment. I'm feeling fine; just frustrated at being cooped up in hospital for at least ten days. As long as I can get some sleep I guess I can cope.

The reason they are keeping me in is, of course, the risk of infection to me and the baby, and then also the risk that I can go into labour at any time with the risk being highest in the first week after the waters have broken. I had a visit from the neonatal unit yesterday explaining the risks of a premature birth as we are only at 29 weeks (30 weeks tomorrow) the risks being the baby's respiration and lung development. I have had the steroid injections to accelerate the baby's lung development so feel more confident about that now.

Another risk (a small risk I am told) for the baby is the risk of bleeding in the brain which can be no big deal or can be dangerous, so if baby is born early, he will go for MRI scans to check for bleeding. I had a tour of the neonatal unit yesterday and the babies were just so little and looked so vulnerable. I would like to keep this little one inside me, as I truly believe it is the best place for him. The risks are minimal as long as we can avoid any infection getting into the membrane, and on a selfish note, the baby being in situ helps me with the effects of the chemo, so it's a win-win situation. If the risks tip either way, I will happily give birth and I honestly believe the baby will be strong enough to cope with the world. He has proved to be a little fighter considering all he has had to face over the past few months. But I will relinquish control to the powers that be in that incredibly invisible way and trust that they have a plan and always know best.

I am learning to trust in a higher power. There is a plan and you need to trust that you are where you are meant to be. Look for the lessons and make sure you act on them.

May 3rd 2007
Let Nature Take Its Course

My last entry was written from my hospital
bed on Wednesday the 25th, although it
was posted later. It is now only a few days
since my last entry and I am still in the
same hospital bed but the situation has
changed so much. Let me fill you in.

Friday morning came and I had had a
good night's sleep. A friend of mine, who
is looking after Laila for me, came to visit
with Laila in the morning. I had a bit of a
headache and didn't have much energy.
Lunchtime arrived and with it, my lunch.
After lunch I started getting a bit of a
tummy cramp and for whatever reason,
my hormones took a tumble and I became
very emotional. I spent the afternoon
crying and sleeping with a headache and
mild cramping that I dismissed as
'something I ate'.

You know when you are premenstrual and
just cry for no apparent reason, and you

have no power to take control or even articulate how you are feeling, and it drains you of every ounce of energy you have in your body? Well, that was me all afternoon.

By late evening I mentioned to Laith on the phone that I was cramping a little so to be warned. I then mentioned it to the midwives and asked for some paracetamol for my headache. They brought the machine to check baby's heart rate and whether I was contracting. The pain then started to kick off, with cold shivers to boot. They took me to the delivery ward to check my progress and by the time I got there I was 8-9 cm dilated. I called Laith in the throes of labour to let him know and was then told to push on my next contraction.

An hour later (at 0:58) and with no reserve energy to speak of (and a lot of excruciating pain) a 3 pound (1.44kg) little baby girl was born naturally and with only scant amounts of gas and air. She needed help breathing initially. As she was ten weeks early, and with all the risk that poses, they whipped her out of me and straight onto a table for checks. As they were about to wheel her off to the Special Care Unit, I asked to see her and vividly remember these very alert little eyes looking back at me. I just knew at that moment that she would be absolutely fine. She was a little fighter with the most incredible determination in her eyes, even at a few minutes old.

I called Laith to let him know. He was in the car park with Laila and they both bundled into the delivery suite a few minutes later. Fortunately the midwife, who Laila got to know as 'Anna Banana', was on hand to make sure all the blood was cleared up and I was decent. Can you imagine the trauma of a little two year old seeing her Mum covered in blood and sweat at 1 o'clock in the morning?

On the way back to the ward we were able to check in on our little miracle baby. She was in her incubator and happily settling into life outside the womb.

So, miracles *do* happen, even when all the odds are stacked against you.

May 3rd 2007
And Life Takes Over

I'm sitting here in my hospital bed with my brain whirring and buzzing all round me. It's been such an information-packed few days that I don't know where to start.

I spent most of the morning in the intensive care unit with baby (Laith and I have hardly seen each other since her birth so have not had a chance to discuss names yet). She is the most contented little soul and so brave.

She was able to breathe on her own a few hours after she was born, which is fantastic for such a little thing, and within a day she had her sucking reflex down pat and has since had a few feeds with a bottle. I am so proud of her. When they feed her through the tube, she instinctively sucks with her mouth, which is a very good sign.

She had to have a lumbar puncture yesterday afternoon as a precaution and apparently she managed that no problem. I wasn't brave enough to be there for it. The cultures from that have come back negative which is brilliant. They are waiting for another culture to be returned before that concern is put to rest.

The Physio department were with baby this morning discussing her little feet. She has a pronounced case of Talipes (club feet) on both her feet. She is going to need full leg plaster casts, which will get changed every week, then a small operation and then boots with a brace for a while. She may have to sleep with the boots on until she is about five. She is going to need all the resolve and strength of character she can muster over the coming few years and a lot of love and support from her family.

She was born on Saturday morning at 0:58. I spent most of that day in bed trying to build up my energy levels and feel vaguely human. Eventually after lunch I mustered all the energy I had to go and see her. I was able to hold her for the first time; which was just incredible. Laith came round with my little Laila on Sunday and it was so nice to see them. Laith got to spend some time with the baby and I got to spend some time with Laila (when she wasn't charming the staff). We took Laila to meet her little sister, and she was so gentle with her, stroking her head and comparing the size of their hands.

I haven't seen Laila since then and it's now Tuesday and I really miss her. I feel guilty for being away from her and also for leaving Laith to just manage everything on his own; although he is more than capable. Then if I go home I am going to feel like I am abandoning the baby. I am still really tired and know I need to sleep and catch up with myself before I plunge into the real world again. Ten days to go before my next chemo so a bit of time to build my strength. I now have two little souls who will keep me focused and determined to get through the next couple of months.

I am beginning to appreciate just how powerful determination can be.

May 5th 2007
Taking A Stand

An update on little one is that she is off the IV fluids now and is getting all her nutrition through her milk. We are trying to get her transferred to our local hospital, which is a five minute drive away. As she is not critical and I have been assured by the staff in the neonatal unit that the care she needs can easily be delivered by my local hospital, I am happy to leave the excellent care of the Homerton.

As for me, my head is feeling a little prickly / sensitive and my hair seems to be thinning a little. Otherwise I feel OK. A bit tired still since the delivery. It's nice being back online and back in touch with friends after a week in hospital.

May 7th 2007
The Big Move

Some good news... Baby may have a cot at our local hospital and may be transferred today, so as soon as Laith is up (it's his turn to sleep in today so I am up with Laila for breakfast) I will get myself ready and head over to the hospital to see her and check that the transfer is going ahead today.

May 8th 2007
Closer To Home

YAY, Baby is one step closer to home. She has been transferred to our local hospital, which is five minutes away from home. And just in time too. I have an appointment tomorrow to get my blood taken and tested ready for the next dose of chemo, and then my chemotherapy on Thursday; so I can go to baby after my appointments, which is fantastic.

I saw her off at the Homerton and then drove over to the Queen Elizabeth and was able to settle her in there. She had some bottle and then settled in and fell asleep. She was making gurgling sounds, which was so nice to hear.

May 10th 2007
The Poison Is Flowing Again.

I had another dose of chemotherapy today. Watching that red liquid coming down the tube and going directly into my veins can be a little scary. It is also very cold and turns my veins and arm quite icy.

It's been about five hours since I finished the treatment and I seem to be reacting very similarly to the previous treatments (which is excellent news). I am feeling OK, perhaps a little light headed, but not significantly so.

When my treatment was over, I headed straight for the baby unit and sat and cuddled little one for about three hours. I love her smell and her closeness. It's so comforting just holding her. A friend who has been through chemo used to go to an art gallery before her treatments as a 'pick me up'. My 'pick me up' are the cuddles I get from my newborn and from Laila at home (and of course, Laith).

It is so important to find something that inspires you that you can do before or after chemotherapy.

May 13th 2007
A New Hair Day

I went for a wig fitting yesterday..... Oh how strange. I was really tired. Laila woke up the previous night at 3 am with a fever and shivering, so after a night of broken sleep and an early wake-up call, I was a bit of a wreck.

Anyway, at the hairdresser, they took me into a little room at the back of the salon and sat me down in front of a mirror. I got a catalogue to look through with Raquel Welch on the cover, staring back at me, looking ever so glamorous. Then came the trying-on.

I must mention that since I gave birth, literally the next day, my hair started thinning and falling out in clumps. I could have stuffed a few pillows or a few stuffed animals with what has already fallen out. It's really annoying, as I can't touch my hair without it filling my hands with wispy strands of hair. Hair everywhere, in the car, in the bed, in the bath, on every carpet, in every bin, on all my clothes, on Laila's hands and clothes, in the food. I'm sick of it. I would rather it was just all gone now so I don't have to see it fall out onto my life and cover it with a carpet of reminders.

I have never tried a wig on before so had no idea really. It was a strange experience. The 'hair' is very shiny and quite abundant. The wigs are thicker and heavier than I imagined. It was quite soul-destroying seeing my thinning and greying hair in between trying on those lush wigs. Anyway, at the end of it all, I chose two to order in, so hopefully in a few days time I can sport a head of thick hair, even though it won't technically be my own.

I would definitely recommend that if your hair is falling out, just shave it off. You don't have to hang on to those reminders.

May 13th 2007
Sunday Night Reflections

I have spent the day with Laith and Laila at Brands Hatch watching a friend race. It was really nice getting out and doing something different for a change. My life seems to revolve around my children and family (which I love) and hospitals, but I do need to break the cycle every so often.

I had a bit of time to reflect and realised just how guilt-ridden this period of my life is. I feel so guilty that I didn't go and see the little one today. When I do see her, I try to be back in time for Laila's bed time or I feel guilty about that. I feel guilty that Laith has had to put his life on hold this year. He was supposed to be out there racing this year, too, and did all the preparation last year for it. I also feel guilty that he has to support the whole family without my help and has been running the household without me while I was in hospital; getting Laila to nursery and himself to work, etc., and I know it isn't an easy task. Just guilt, guilt, guilt. I need to get over it. It's not good for me and isn't going to make me get any better.

As for the chemo, I am feeling OK generally. I'm not really sure what I'm supposed to be feeling, except normal. I guess that's a good thing really, no self-fulfilling prophecies of feeling ill.

I am starting to realize that guilt is a natural and common emotion that rears its head when you have to take time out for yourself during treatment. The guilt of not contributing, the guilt of putting your loved ones through this ordeal, etc. But it's not a constructive emotion and it eats away at your strength. Take the time to reframe this experience, i.e., 'This is a life lesson we all need to learn from.' or 'Perhaps I have been neglecting to take that time out for myself and now it's been imposed on me.' Whatever works for your situation.

May 16th 2007
Counting Blessings

I spent this afternoon in the Special Care Baby Unit, just holding my little girl. She is out of the incubator now and in a cot, and that is brilliant. They are weighing her tonight so will have her new weight tomorrow. She is doing so well. All the staff say how good she is. She also had a hearing test and her hearing is perfect.

There is a little boy in a cot next to baby's. His three big brothers and Dad were there yesterday to visit him. I hear today that his Mum had passed away giving birth to him; leaving dad with four boys to raise. Again, I count my blessings.

Laila has picked up a cold from nursery and I seem to have picked it up from her. My body is fighting tooth and nail to keep me well, but it is sapping every ounce of energy out of me. I am so knackered. I can't get enough sleep. I came home yesterday after dropping Laila off at nursery and slept for three hours. I am ready to collapse into bed again (and have been since about 5 pm). I'm also a bit hormonal and emotional today. I guess it's because I'm so tired.

It is important to realize that there is always someone worse off than you are. Count your blessings.

May 19th 2007
And The Poison Kicks In

Just a quick one to say I'm feeling bloody awful. I have a sore throat that feels like a burning hot poker has been shoved down it, a headache to match and a sore and red eye. I thought this was all symptoms of a cold I picked up from Laila but it seems (after reading the literature from the chemo treatment suite) these are side effects from the chemo. The full force of the poison has kicked in. What a difference from the last two chemo treatments when I had no side effects at all. I also have NO energy for anything. It feels like the plug has been pulled from the energy source. My electricity has gone.

I am also losing my mind a little. I forget things all the time. If I don't do things straight away, I forget I need to do them and only remember again when I see them or it's too late.

I am sure it can get a lot worse and I'm really hoping it doesn't. I don't do 'sick' well. I'm really struggling.

It's amazing how powerful your body system is. Your body will protect and preserve itself. If it needs to limit certain functions in order to have the strength to deal with the drugs, it will. Don't be too harsh on yourself. Write everything down if you have to.

May 20th 2007
Good Old Garlic

I woke up this morning with my sore throat having travelled up to my ears and now my ears are really sore too. I can't get hold of my GP on a Sunday or my oncologist, so I decided to have some raw garlic for breakfast. As my sense of taste is about 60% gone and my sense of smell about 90% gone, it has been no problem. I'm feeling better for it.

Here is the little one, on my lap, fast asleep.

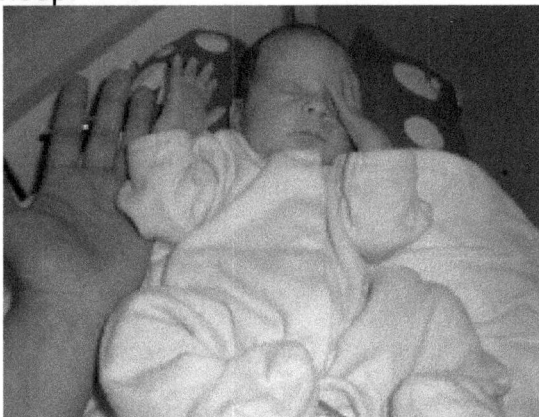

And another picture of the little one.

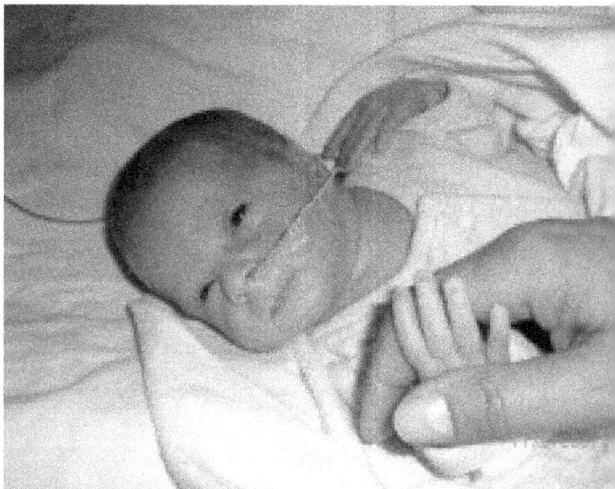

May 23rd 2007
Thoughts For The Day

I have been 'off line' for a couple of days. Mainly, I have not been feeling well with my sore throat and then an ear infection (which is still bugging me) and just being exhausted.

Please don't think that I am taking this lying down. I have a whole lot of fight in me and I am tackling this by taking the bull by the horns. I often don't write about the fight as it's a daily attitude. It's when I'm a little introspective, or something hits a chord that I write about it and these things are generally things I regret or am upset about. I am nearly halfway through this battle (at least the chemo bit) and in my mind I do not have cancer anymore; it was removed when the lump was removed. This treatment is described by my oncologist as my insurance policy and that's the way I look at it. I have many good years ahead of me and intend to see my children grow up and fuss over my grandchildren. *It's all about the attitude*.

I spent this morning at the hospital with the little one. Her weight on Sunday night was 1.96, which is brilliant as when she reaches 2kg, and then she has reached a milestone criteria for letting her come home.

The other criteria are her being able to breath without oxygen, which she hasn't been on since the day she was born. Being able to take her feeds by bottle, which she is managing more of each day, although not quite there yet. And she needs to be past 34 weeks gestation time, which she will be on Thursday. The doctors mentioned on Monday that she may be able to come home next week if all the criteria are met. I honestly can't wait but am also apprehensive as I am so exhausted a lot of the time. But I will cope as always.

While sitting in the baby unit, the other Mums will come in and breast feed their little ones. Many find it difficult, as the babies may not latch on as they should or aren't sucking. I have also heard a lot of Mums complaining and often disliking the whole process of breastfeeding. Hearing Mums say that they don't want to keep it up as they don't like the maternity bras and miss their push up bras (which I can understand). This all breaks my heart.

I feel so cheated out of being able to breastfeed my baby. While holding her, if she is getting hungry, she will route toward me for milk and it breaks my heart that I cannot offer her the comfort and nutrition I should naturally be able to. Instinctively I yearn to just whip my boobs out and feed her but know I will be doing her more harm than good. I guess a bottle and cuddles are the next best thing.

An important point to take away from this is to celebrate even the small challenges in your life. There are people out there who cannot do the things you are doing.

May 25th 2007
Spirits Are Lifting

For the first time in what feels like absolutely ages, I am feeling vaguely energetic and back to normal. My ear is still blocked so I can't hear very well, but at least nothing hurts.

I think we will spend as much of the weekend as the weather permits in the garden and getting things ready for baby. She will be home within a week or two and we have absolutely nothing ready (including her name).

May 27th 2007
It's Sunday Night Again And I'm Reflecting

I'm absolutely exhausted but for all the right reasons this time. Laith and a friend of mine were in cahoots all of last week and arranged for me to go out last night as a surprise (I don't get out that often). Well it was fun. We had dinner at a Mexican restaurant in Blackheath and then went on to a 'disco' downstairs. It was great. We danced and had a wonderful time catching up. Thank you both so much.

I returned home at 1am and while washing my face, I heard a noise outside and looked out of the window to find a bloke in the process of lifting one of our fence panels and stealing Laith's push bike. I woke Laith up, but all too late so we are one bike down (again). It's enough to put one off people.

Laila was up at 6 am and seeing as we only got to bed at 3 am, I'm shattered.

I went to see baby today and she is now taking ALL her feeds by bottle. They have taken the tube out of her nose, which is brilliant news. They weigh her tonight so will have an update on that tomorrow. She is doing so well and she should be home soon (this week perhaps). I can't wait.

What awful weather. Rain, rain, and rain... perhaps the sun will come out tomorrow...

June 1st 2007
It's Been Three Weeks Already ... And Another Cup Of Poison

Yes, it's been one hell of a week. Laila has been off nursery (they closed for half term) so I have been a full time Mum (which I have enjoyed, actually). On Tuesday I called the hospital to find out how the little one was doing and was told she had been swabbed and the swabs came back as positive for MRSA (Methicillin-resistant Staphylococcus aureus). It's not what I wanted to hear and panic set in but after asking a lot of questions, it seems it is not in her blood so she is fine. They are treating her eyes and nose and bathing her in special bath stuff to fix it. Laila and I had swabs done on Wednesday morning and I called today and our swabs are negative, so we are OK.

On Wednesday I had to go to the hospital to get my blood taken and tested again for the chemo on Thursday. Laila came with me and that tested all my patience and skill in parenting. She was as good as gold; seeing as we were at the doctors at 8:30 am, then straight on to the hospital and we only left there after 2 pm, and she hadn't had lunch. She spent some time with her little sister and was brilliant stroking her and holding her bottle and patting her on her back, as well as giving her a few very tight hugs which had me stressed out but I think she will make a FANTASTIC big sister.

On Thursday I dropped Laila off with a friend while I went off to have my chemo. It was my fourth treatment and marked the halfway point in my chemo. It took three attempts to get a line into my arm/hand but finally the last of the red stuff entered my body. I felt a bit 'woozy' afterwards; not much energy but able to drive and fetch Laila. Fortunately Laith brought home two pizzas for dinner so that saved me doing any cooking.

Today I woke up shattered, not able to open my eyes or wrench myself up from the bed but Laith had to get to work so I got up (eventually). My cheeks were flushed and hot. It felt like I was sitting centimetres away from a very hot radiator. That lasted most of the day but eventually faded away. I think I might get into the garden tomorrow. I need to get a compost bin and some compost and then I can get some more flowers in and perhaps even a vegetable patch (although I know it's late in the season to start a vegetable patch). At the moment, I'm feeling OK, considering.

June 6th 2007
Home At Last

At last, baby is coming home. We had a meeting at the hospital this afternoon with all the people involved in her care (present and future) and we are set to bring her home tomorrow. She is also on demand feeding now (as opposed to scheduled feeding) and her weight is 2.3 kg, which is nearly double her birth weight.

Baby has an appointment on Friday to get her feet assessed and then next Thursday she is getting her first plaster casts done. It was going to be tomorrow but as she is only getting out of the hospital then, it was rescheduled for next week.

Everything is ready for her arrival. We have the cot ready with all her clothes and blankets and muslins washed in non-bio detergent. Her pram and car seat and carrier are also washed and ready to pick her up. I can't wait. Time to get settled and into a routine at home and start living as a family of four.

As for me, I'm fine. My hair is sparse (just about 70 or 80% lost) and it is hard to see myself in the mirror with bits of my scalp showing. I am most comfortable with my hat or a scarf on and would sleep with one on if it would stay put.

Otherwise, I'm feeling OK. Laith is working hard and is still at work now. We had another break-in on Saturday, so that's taking it toll on us. Laith has been very calm and mature about the break-in's. He has matured a lot in the last two years and it is a steady progression of maturity; and I'm loving the man emerging. I've always loved his wild spirit and that's still there. It's just more appropriately placed somehow.

I absolutely believe that challenges are sent to help us grow and mature as people.

June 8th 2007
A Name For A Little Princess

It's been a busy day (baby's first day at home). Laila doesn't go to nursery on Fridays so I've had both of them all day and I must admit I was a little daunted by that but we have had a brilliant day.

Laila has been fantastic. She is so gentle and caring about her new little sister and wants to hug and kiss her all the time. Baby has kept her occupied all day which has been fantastic.

I think it has been decided (by chance) that baby may be called Ruby. It is a toss up between two names; Ruby or Roxanne. We have asked Laila which name she prefers and now she is convinced that she has two sisters, one called Ruby (at home with us now) and another called Roxanne (or as she says, 'Roxand') who is still in hospital. No matter how we try to explain it, she is having none of it.

I'm still fine. I should be in bed as Ruby/Roxanne will need a feed at some point during the night.

June 10th 2007
Out With The Old And In With The New
(Even If It <u>Is</u> Fake!)

It's been an interesting weekend. I went to the hairdresser to fetch my wig on Saturday. I ended up with an interesting new mop of hair on my head.

As for my natural locks... well, there is not much left of that (and it pains me to look at it). I had the best of intentions of shaving it all off this weekend but didn't quite manage to get round to it. Instead I spent today in the garden weeding and planting beautiful flowers.

I read in a book once that as a therapy for cancer, some lady would weed her garden and imagine she was weeding the cancer cells and tumours out of her body and when planting anything, she would imagine creative thoughts and ideas being planted in her. I really like that idea and do believe in the power of the imagination when it comes to healing the body and mind.

It's been great having Ruby home this weekend. She spent today asleep in the shade, in the garden. She is such a good little girl.

Laila is still fantastic with Ruby and really just wants to hug her all the time. We have to keep telling her to leave Ruby alone so she can get some sleep.

A lesson to take away from today's entry must be to use your imagination. It is through our imagination that we communicate with our consciousness and we are able to direct it by what we choose to imagine.

June 15th 2007
Birthday Blues

It was my birthday yesterday and it's not one I would like to remember. I had an appointment to take Ruby for her casts (she has severe Talipes, or club feet). I have had all the literature and knew what was going to happen but I just wasn't prepared for her gut-wrenching crying. It tore right through me and I came home and spent the rest of the day in tears.

The casts are really heavy. I'm sure they must be about as heavy as she is. She is not particularly comfortable but is getting used to them (and so am I).

Laith has been busy doing stuff around the house and for not much reason. Today he blitzed the house and tidied madly (of course I was suspicious). He then disappeared and came home with Laila's cousins who have come to visit from Wales for the weekend. One of them we hadn't seen since Laila was three months old. It was such a fantastic surprise but I think there is more to come tomorrow. Laith is renowned for surprising me.

June 18th 2007
Party Time

I was right... Laith sent me out to buy a new outfit on Saturday morning and then a friend arranged to take Laila and I to the park for an hour or so. When we arrived back home, there was all sorts of chaos on the go. Banners on the walls saying 'Happy Birthday' and loads of balloons; and then all my friends started arriving with gifts and children and all sorts. It was great. Some of them I hadn't seen in a good while and it was fantastic that so many people made all the effort to be there. I wore my new wig and got lots of really positive feedback.

Thanks to Laith, my shining star, for arranging a brilliant birthday bash, and thanks to all his collaborators and to all the people for making the effort to be there and for all the lovely gifts for myself and Ruby and Laila.

I have my next chemo on Thursday. It's the first of the new drug so it will be interesting to see how I react to it.

Do you like my lovely new wig??

June 26th 2007
The Poison With A Sting In Its Tail...

I haven't been blogging for a while now. To be honest, with a little soul at home demanding feeding every three hours (night and day) it's been difficult to find the time.

Last week was a logistics nightmare. I had blood taken on Wednesday. I took Ruby with me and of course she made all heads turn. All was good to go for Thursday.

We had to get Laila to nursery on Thursday morning, then back to soak Ruby in a bath to get her casts off. I expected it to take a while, but it took forever and with Ruby's appointment scheduled for 11 am and my chemo appointment set for 10:30 am, we resorted to a pair of scissors and cut the casts off. Laith and I were both soaking but relieved to have her free. Laith then dropped me off and took Ruby for her new casts.

The chemo went in easily. I was fine until Sunday, when I started feeling sluggish. Monday hit me hard. I was totally grounded. I had Laila home and was barely able to move. Today was marginally better but still feeling shattered and in pain. It's like my body has been gently beaten with a rolling pin. It affects my whole body and also my organs. It also feels like there is a steam train racing around my veins. I haven't been sociable at all and all I really want to do is curl up in a ball and wake up when it's all over.

July 8th 2007
Time Passes So Quickly

It's been a while since I last wrote. Since my last chemo I had ten days of feeling rotten. I have a sore body both outside and in as well as ulcers and sore fingers. I'm not looking forward to my next three sessions of the same drug. This is not a fairground ride I would like to stay on, thank you.

I have been feeling better for about a week now but have my next chemo this coming week so I am just enjoying feeling normal for a while.

I have been thinking about what I want to do next year after all of this is over. I am finding this quite a positive experience. All my insecurities of not doing things that challenge me more than I am comfortable with are being tested and I am finding myself wanting the challenges. It's like I have wasted so much of my life not wanting to do things. Perhaps my new motto should be 'a challenge a day keeps the cancer away'.

I am now also officially bald. There was so little hair left that I eventually asked Laith to just shave it off; and it's fantastic, if a little cold. I still wear my wig out in public and am getting used to it.

The girls are well. Laila has turned into a little girl all of a sudden. She is such fun to be with and is as bright as a button. Ruby is growing and is able to turn herself over now, casts and all. She had her immunizations last Monday and has been high maintenance ever since. I do feel sorry for her. She isn't feeling well.

Laith is well. We are both tired due to waking at night to feed Ruby (and she can holler when she gets the chance). Other than that, he is working hard and not taking enough time out for himself so becomes stressed.

July 11th 2007
Reality Really Bites

That time has arrived again. I can't believe it has been three weeks already. Ruby and I went to the hospital this morning to get my blood tested and to have a consult with my oncologist.

Admittedly, I was tired from Ruby feeding all hours of the morning. I was sitting in the waiting room chatting to one of the other ladies who has her treatments at the same time as me, so we have long chats when we're there. Another lady waiting for her treatment joined in with the conversation (on how the treatment affected us). It turns out she has been treated for the past six years. She didn't find the lump in her breast, and a secondary cancer developed in her liver and this recurs every few years. She looks so well and has such a positive disposition that's nice to see after all she is going through. Her husband and I were chatting and he was saying that it is very trying for them and especially him. It really does affect the people around you more than it does you.

As we were chatting, a young girl walked past who has a tumour on her brain which is inoperable. She looks about 25. She has been fighting the cancer for a few years too, and it's getting worse as she now has epileptic fits. My heart goes out to her.

Then another woman was wheeled in by her husband and teenage daughter. She looked very frail. Apparently she is a doctor and had been well enough to be working part time a week ago, and then suddenly things all went downhill for her. I'm not sure what cancer she has but it reminded me of how fragile life can be and that cancer kills and it could so easily be me in that wheelchair. It was a stark reminder that there is a bitter reality behind this disease and I really need to count my lucky stars and view each day as a gift to be cherished. I have shed a few tears today thinking of her.

Again, it's a reminder that there are always others worse off than you. Count your blessings.

July 12th 2007
What A Day...

It's been one hell of a day. Ruby and I went to the hospital for another dose of poison. They only make it up when I get there as it's expensive and has a short shelf life, so we had to wait a while before we were called in. We arrived at 11:30 am.

It took a while once we were called in to get going, but at least the line (needle) went in first time today which was a huge bonus (it usually takes three goes and it's bloody sore). It's definitely the worst part of getting the chemo and I had a sleepless night recently worrying over the lines going in.

The drip was going in quite nicely and I was engrossed in a conversation when all of a sudden I had a hot flush starting from my belly and ending up in my head. I was struggling to breath and felt nauseous and faint with my head rushing. I was powerless to do anything, I couldn't even speak. Fortunately the lady I was speaking to had the presence of mind to tell the nurses on duty. They stopped the drug and switched the fan on me until I felt better. Apparently it's a fairly common reaction and the body's way of telling me it doesn't like the drug. They slowed the drip down and I tolerated the rest of the drug with no problems. Ruby and I left at 4 pm eventually. I called Laith to come home and fetch Laila from nursery, as I didn't feel good about driving. I gave Ruby her milk, put her to sleep and went and sat outside in the fresh air for a while.

I am still flushed but feeling so much better. Hopefully the steroids, which I get after every chemotherapy session, won't affect me too badly this time round.

July 17th 2007
How I Would Love To Get Off This Ride

It's been five days since the chemo, and I'm feeling rough. My body is aching and my legs are really sore. The joints (knees and hips and ankles) are painful and I feel very unsure of my steps. Another side effect is painful fingertips and nails, so doing the washing up (baby bottles, etc.) is torture. Yet another side effect is sore gums. It feels like the inside of my mouth has pins and needles and parts of the gums are getting raw. I also can't taste food, which is pretty boring.

I have been feeling disorientated at times too. Ruby woke for her 3am feed the other night. I didn't hear her and Laith had to wake me up to get her. I then had her in the bed on my chest and must have dosed off. Amidst dreams and hallucinations, I was convinced there were five screaming babies on the bed and I didn't know what to do. I was really stressed out for about half an hour until I came to my senses and took control of the situation. It was pretty scary… Ruby slept through it all so she wasn't stressed out in the least.

Laith has gone away on a business trip and so it's me and the girls at home. I feel awful not having the energy to do much with Laila. Ruby sleeps much of the time so is much easier to cope with. Hopefully my Mum should be here soon to help and support me for a while until this nightmare is over.

July 20th 2007
Ruby

We changed Ruby's casts on Thursday. She was really good for her first leg but when we started the second leg she kicked off and nothing on earth could pacify her. For the rest of Thursday afternoon Ruby just wouldn't settle. She was fractious with her feeds and just kept crying. This went on all night so we were up every hour or so trying to comfort her.

This morning I called the physiotherapists and their advice was to get the casts off; which we spent all afternoon doing. Once we had done the first leg (the one we did last when putting the casts on that she was so upset about) she just calmed down.

Looking at both legs, there was a patch on each leg where the skin was rubbing off, so no wonder she was so upset. Poor little thing. She had some milk and fell straight to sleep. I'm looking forward to a better night's sleep tonight and a happier little girl.

July 29th 2007
Getting It Together

It's Sunday morning and the house is quiet. Laith has gone to visit some friends with Laila and I am here alone with Ruby (who is sleeping).

My Mum will be here on Tuesday and I am really looking forward to it. We haven't seen each other in almost three years so it will be as much a reunion as a visit. Laila is also looking forward to 'Granny Merle' coming to visit.

I am feeling OK, just really exhausted, which I think is a combination of the chemo and also having to get up to feed Ruby every two to three hours through the night, so just not getting enough sleep. It's chemo again this coming week and not looking forward to that, but it is my second to last one, so another step in the right direction. I can't wait for my life to return to some degree of normality once the treatment is over. Roll on November.

August 2nd 2007
The Poison Chalice Revisited

It's that time again. Yes, another cup of poison. It's been a long day. My appointment was for 11am but the ward was very short- staffed due to school holidays and there was only one person on duty (Lisa, our hero) so my appointment was delayed until 2 pm. I was due to fetch Laila at 5 o'clock so they started me as soon as I got there. Within ten minutes I had another reaction to the drug. Not as bad as the last time but enough to leave me light-headed. My lungs tightened up, my heart raced, I started coughing and I felt light-headed and hot. They slowed the drug down to run for two hours. I ended up leaving at 5 pm. Laith came and picked me up at the hospital, which was a godsend.

The next appointment will be my last and I can't wait. My chalice of poison is nearly empty and my body can bear testimony to that. Let's hope that this really will be the last.

August 10th 2007
Mum's The Word

It's been an exhausting week. After the chemo last week I had a day or two of feeling OK (thanks to the steroids) then a slump, like someone had pulled the plug. I also had the pains in my body from the withdrawal of the steroids but that lasted only a day or two.

There seems to be a pattern. If I exert myself at all (like taking a gentle walk to the park with Laila) then the next day I hit an energy low. I rest, and then the next day I have some energy again. Then I do stuff and the cycle continues. I have a new respect for energy. Things I would normally have taken for granted, like being able to go to the park or on an outing with my family, renders me useless the next day. I want my battery back.

My Mum is here for a few months and having her here is a godsend. She is fantastic and a real help all round. She is getting used to handling babies again and is good with little Ruby. Laila loves having Granny Merle here. Mum is really good in the garden too, so she is helping me sort ours out; which is very exciting.

My hair is growing back and is a few millimetres long now. It's white and hardly shows at all. My eyelashes and eyebrows have thinned dramatically and haven't stopped thinning yet. My nails are doing OK and my fingers haven't been as sore this time round (yet). My sense of taste hasn't been affected as badly this time either.

I realize how important it is not to let this disease take over my life. Laith has been brilliant by not letting me forget that and not really allowing it to change our normality. Naturally there are exceptions occasionally but life goes on as normal and this allows me to feel and act normally. If I were to take myself out of my normal day-to-day life I would reinforce to myself that things are different; and to be honest, I would probably start to feel sorry for myself, which can very easily spiral down into some degree of depression.

Here's to life lived as normally and fully as possible.

I guess a lesson here is not to push yourself too hard. Conserve your energy and use it sparingly. Ask yourself if doing that activity is worth a day of not being able to do anything at all. Also, don't change your routine too much. It provides a sense of normality in your life. If you let that go, it is just too easy to let everything else go. Keep your standards up and a sense of normality.

August 19th 2007
Time Out

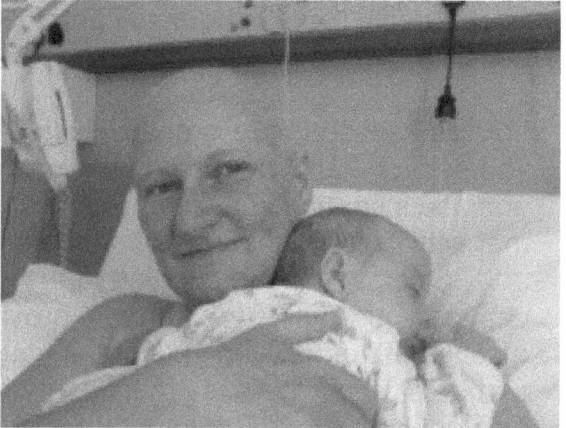

It feels like I have been on an extended holiday over the past week. Actually I have been in hospital with low neutrophils (Low white blood count, so no immune system, thanks to the chemo). Last Sunday night I was feeling a bit grotty. I had been feeling like I was getting a cold but just figured it was a side effect of the chemo. I had also picked up a sore throat (everyone here is coughing). Anyway, after Ruby's feed at 3 am, I went into the bathroom and took my temperature. It was 38.1. Our instructions are that if our temperature ever hits 38, we must go straight into hospital. It was 3 o'clock in the morning and I wasn't going to wake Laith up to take me into A&E, so I went back to bed to nurse my fever.

Monday morning, I took my temperature again and it was 37.3, so I figured crisis over. I called the chemo nurses anyway, just in case. They told me to come in and get my bloods checked out. With one thing and another, it was the afternoon before I managed to find the time to go to the hospital. My chemotherapy nurse, Joanne, told me off for delaying but told me to come in straight away. I got my bloods done and went home. Joanne called me when she got my results and told me to go straight to A&E. I did. They gave me intravenous antibiotics within an hour and after loads of questions and loads of prodding and five hours later, they had a bed for me on the cancer ward. I was put into isolation as my neutrofils were dangerously low and all possible risk of infection was a danger to my health. Everyone coming into my room had to wear an apron and gloves and when Laith and my Mum and the kids came to visit, they all had to wear masks too. They all went to see the GP on the Tuesday and were advised not to come and see me as it was too dangerous to my health (I will have to thank him for that next time I see him!!!) Not.

So I spent the week watching TV and reading. Not being allowed out of my room and with few visitors (big thanks to Cherry and Florrie, my Mum and Ruby). Fortunately Tracy (a fellow patient) had been admitted a day before I was so we were at least able to speak to each other via phone as she was in the same boat as me. A big thanks to Tracy for the magazines and newspapers and excellent company.

It is nice to be home now. I missed my family. Mum and Laith are well and did a good job of keeping things together for the girls. Ruby has grown and Laila is my little star. We spent some time today cuddled in her bed reading her new books, we also had a bath together and I lay with her until she was asleep. It is full on but that's my life and I wouldn't have it any other way.

It is so important to check your temperature and act if there is a problem. My oncologist told me that people don't die from chemotherapy; they can however die from an infection contracted when their immune system is down.

September 4th 2007
Out On A Limb

I have been very lax at writing but there are never enough hours in a day. Last week I went to the hospital for my last course of chemo. I had my blood taken on Wednesday, and then headed up to the Macmillan Suite for my appointment with my oncologist. He called me into his office and after a brief chat, he told me that NICE have changed the protocol on the chemotherapy and instead of recommending four courses of docetaxel, they are recommending only three, so effectively my chemotherapy is over and had been for almost a month. I was rendered speechless.

This decision was based on research, which suggested that the side effects of the drug (including cardio and infection risk) did not warrant the fourth dose, as the drug was strong enough within the three doses to do its job. The whole thing has left me a little nervous and feeling as though I have been shoved out of the family home after a lifetime of security. I know that I have a direct line back to the hospital in case I need it and I have already made use of that lifeline. I am trying to get my radiotherapy moved forward so I can spend some more time with my Mum towards the end of her stay.

I love having my Mum here. I still have very little energy on a day to day basis. Mum is a great help all round and is getting on well with the girls (especially little Ruby) Laila can be a challenge at the best of times and requires a little management (as do all three-year-olds, I'm sure). I am really going to miss my Mum.

Ruby has her operation scheduled for Friday. The doctors at Kings College Hospital will work their magic and do some keyhole surgery on her feet to lengthen her tendons at the back of her legs. It's very exciting (because it's a milestone for us) and scary at the same

time. She will be fine and is growing so quickly at the moment.
It's Laila's birthday party in two week's time. I'm not sure I have the energy to bake cakes and make loads of food from scratch, so I guess it will be finger food and M&S cake all round. I can't believe my little girl is going to be three years old.

My hair is growing back but will be a while before I can bare my crowning glory to the unsuspecting public.

I have realized that the supportive environment of the hospital is a safe and friendly place to be. Everyone is so nice. It can become addictive as it fills a need in us. There is a possibility that you may keep yourself ill just to stay in that environment. I had to find another way of fulfilling that need in order to feel safe out of that environment. An absolutely crucial part of my recovery process.

September 7th 2007
It's Been A Long Day

Just a quick entry to mention that little Ruby had her operation this afternoon. She is nineteen weeks old and has now been through two operations, two biopsies and had chemotherapy in utero. One month in Special Care Baby Unit (half of which was in an incubator) Full leg casts re-applied weekly and now an operation under local anaesthetic. She has endured a lifetime of medical intervention during her short little life.

She was so brave. I volunteered Laith to take Ruby into theatre. The operation took all of half an hour under local anaesthetic. Laith came out with tears in his eyes. Apparently Ruby cried when they made the incisions. Poor little thing. And I do feel for Laith having to watch and comfort his youngest little princess through it all.

September 20th 2007
Happy Birthday Little Angel!

I haven't written for a while because there hasn't been much to say. My energy levels are just about back to normal. My hair is growing. There is still too much skin showing so I am still wearing a wig unless at home.

It was Laila's birthday party last weekend and we had a fantastic day of food and drink and cake and bouncy castles.

I start my radiotherapy on Monday, which consists of a gruelling four and a half week cycle, but then I get my life back and we can go on holiday. Roll on November.

September 24th 2007
The Beginning Of The End

Today was the beginning of the end of my journey. I started my radiotherapy today. I woke up late and had to rush out of the door without any breakfast so by the time I got there, I was desperately lacking in concentration.

After a short chat about what was going to happen, I was ushered into a changing room to sport my new, dashing hospital gown (which I get to take home with me). I then waited to be called into the radiotherapy room. I was then told to take off my shoes and get onto the bed placing my feet on the board at the bottom. They then moved me in millimetres and drew on me and the huge radiotherapy machine waltzed around me and took photos and measurements. There is a picture on the ceiling above the bed of a beach and palm trees. Is that supposed to make me feel better? Then they left me alone to do the radiotherapy. I couldn't help but wonder what the hell I was doing there, all alone in this sterile, freezing cold room.

It was all over in minutes (very cold minutes). I got dressed and left. I headed straight for a coffee and a Chelsea bun. On my way home, I stopped and bought a magazine. In it there was an article about three women who had survived breast cancer, and their stories. I read it on the train and it had me in tears, just bringing back memories of chemo and the relationships this illness affects. I'm on the home straight now and am looking forward to a long life of health and prosperity.

I'm beginning to understand that cancer doesn't have to be a death sentence. There are many survivors and it's by speaking to them that you learn to become one yourself.

October 1st 2007
Let's Run With It...

I have set myself a new challenge; I am planning to do the 'Race for Life' run in 2008 for Cancer Research UK. I am recruiting as many people as I can to do the race with me to raise awareness and money for cancer research and care. This is my focus for 2008.

My body and mind have been to hell and back this year and now that I am feeling a little better, and my energy levels are on the up, I need to get myself fit and strong and healthy.

December 24th 2007
At Long Last

Well, my treatments are all finished now and life carries on. My hair is growing back. It came out a striking 'salt and pepper' colour, which was great fun initially, but I just felt I am too young to be grey, so I dyed it and now I'm a delicious blond. I will be becoming a luscious red head soon.

It's lovely having eyebrows and eyelashes and a hairline again. The rest could quite happily have stayed away but unfortunately all the other hair on my body is back with a vengeance. Back to plucking and shaving and waxing... My nails are just starting to get back to normal too.

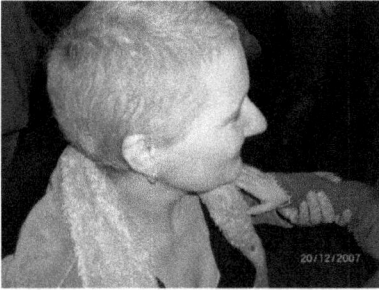

In an attempt to fully re-engage with my life, I have found a job for two days a week. I'm so excited about it. It's been three and a half years since I last worked in an office and I'm really relishing the time in an adult environment using my intellect and just doing normal things.

The girls are both well. Ruby is eating us out of house and home and Laila had her first nativity play in which she was a robin. I was so proud of her. She did such a good job and brought tears to our eyes.

Laith is also well. He is taking two weeks off work to recharge and relax before a busy 2008. Hopefully we will be going away for a while.

I am going to the gym, in training for the 'Race For Life'. It's fantastic having the energy, even just to run 1 km. I'm also swimming which I'm LOVING although I only manage two or three laps at a time between short breaks.

Family life is running me off my feet. But I am well and embracing life and trying to get back to some sort of normality after a year of chaos. I am open to all sorts of wonderful new experiences and bear no malice or resentment in my heart. My life starts now and I intend to make the most of it.

I've discovered that swimming is brilliant for strengthening your muscles after an operation. My arm has been on about sixty percent capacity and with the swimming is very quickly returning to normal use.

February 2nd 2008
Moving On...

Life seems to have swept me up and my feet have barely touched the ground since my treatment finished. My hair is growing back beautifully and I am starting to feel a bit more like 'myself' for the first time in a long, long time.

I have been going to the gym (time permitting and not nearly as often as I would like) but my fitness levels are creeping up which is brilliant. I have given myself a goal to work towards. I am signed up to run the 'Race for Life' to raise money for cancer research.

If last year taught me anything, it would have to be that we NEED challenges in our lives in order to keep ourselves sane and ultimately, healthy. We need to achieve too; it keeps our energy vibrating and our self-esteem intact and it means we can walk tall with our heads held high.

These things are vital to our physical health in the long run.

So, challenge yourself daily. It keeps you happy, healthy, achieving and energetic and is great for self esteem.

February 15th 2009
No Time For Regret

Life is, well life, really. I am living day to day, pretty much as I always have; I just have more hair this year. I have spent a lot of time last year coming to terms with what had happened to me and just dealing with the anger and fear that took over with my cancer diagnosis. I have dealt with a lot of emotional baggage that I have been carrying around for most of my life and the whole process has been cathartic. I feel as though I am still in the emergence stage, a bit like coming out of a cocoon. I have done a lot of necessary emotional 'house work' and although I still feel I have some work to do, I am emerging, a new person, and I like her a lot more than I did the one that stepped into that cocoon in 2007.

It is important to me that the people closest to me learn to trust in me again. Perhaps trust is not the right word. Let me try to explain. I think that my diagnosis put a lot of pressure onto those closest to me. Suddenly I was not able to contribute as I always had; on so many levels. I was out of 'circulation' all year in 2007 due to treatment and then dealing with the effects of the treatment, and the emotional rollercoaster and the 'causes' took up the whole of 2008. My family thought they were getting me back last year and I wasn't able to be there for them. It has been hard on all of us but I am emerging from this madness and ready to embrace life.

One thing I have realized is that life is short and there is no time to be unhappy, or stuck doing something you don't feel good about. Make those moves, take those chances and grab life with both hands. There is no time for regret.

It is becoming evident to me that when the treatment is over, the recovery process starts. Emotionally I was in a very dark place. Take time to work through what you need to in order to connect with yourself. Only then can you truly connect with others.

Life is too precious to take for granted. There is no time to be unhappy. Take action to create the life of your dreams.

May 13th 2009
Visiting An Old Haunt...

It's a funny old world we live in. I have emerged from my cocoon and am spreading my wings, realizing the opportunities that are there for the taking and life is good, better than I ever remember it.

Then something happens to focus my attention on where I have come from. My Mum is diagnosed with breast cancer and is having a mastectomy at the end of May. She is so far away but speaking to her on the phone, I realize that she is taking a ride on the very same rollercoaster that I spent so much time on two years ago. It is difficult to be aware of what she is going through; it feels like I am revisiting an old haunt, but obviously a necessary thing for me to be doing at the moment.

Afterword

This is a very sketchy account of my journey through the treatment of breast cancer and a rather unconventional pregnancy. After the treatment 'treadmill', I found myself in a place that was devastatingly stark and unpleasant. I somehow managed to find myself at the bottom of a huge pit. It felt as though I had been buried alive, on my own, with no way out. I remember feeling completely shut off from the world. It was dark, as though I was in an underground tunnel with no escape. I shut myself down and just switched myself off, severing any human ties I had. I was still 'living' with my family but had closed myself off emotionally from them to protect them from the inevitable 'death from cancer' that I was convinced was going to happen very soon, although I had been given the all clear.

During this time, from October 2007 until March 2008, I remember feeling so desperate that I was on the verge of leaving my family (on more than one occasion) and disappearing from their lives forever because I couldn't handle the emotional demands and didn't feel alive or that I belonged. To me it felt as though I would be doing them a favour. Just imagine, for a second, how desperate I was to even contemplate leaving my partner of nine years and my two young children.

I watched a film recently and I remember a line that said, 'You have to break them down in order to build them up.' which I completely identify with. At this stage I was broken right down. My turning point came when I was encouraged to go to a weekend workshop. The person that went in to that workshop on the Friday and the person that emerged on the Sunday were two very different people.

This is where my life started to changed and the healing journey began, and it has been (and still is) an incredible journey. The insights from this workshop and all of the healing tools I have gathered will change your thinking about illness and wellness and allow you to create the life you choose.

The emotional recovery process started with the weekend seminar. This was my 'journey of self discovery' which is so important when you are trying to sort things out. It was extremely uncomfortable wading around in my 'stuff' but it was also the most empowering thing I have ever done.

My next step was to study the tools and techniques which allow for these changes. But it's not just about the tools, it is a mindset. I needed to look at the world in a different way to how I had been doing it all my life. This created a massive shift in consciousness for me. Realizing the power in how you view your circumstances has been life-changing.

I now understand the link between lifestyle and disease and have been fortunate to have people around me who have helped me to construct a lifestyle that supports health and vitality. I am now in a place where I honestly have to remind myself that I have had cancer. I am stronger and healthier and happier than I have ever been. I am more comfortable with who I am now.

The best part is that I am still the same person I always was. I am not in denial or kidding myself that life is perfect and I will never experience any challenges. I am now in a place where I know that I can handle those challenges. I am still learning every day and am open to new information. I actively seek it. I am happy, healthy and looking forward to a long and incredible life.

I feel as though I have a secret that I want to share and that chapter starts here.

About Cancer Coach

Cancer Coach is a concept based around the cancer journey and most importantly the recovery process of cancer patients. There are very specific circumstances that contribute to the cause of cancer and without addressing these circumstances; we leave ourselves vulnerable to disease.

Cancer Coach helps you to deal with the circumstances of your illness and the emotions that are overwhelming you right now and together we will co-create the Mindset and Lifestyle that will move you forward into your future with clarity and ease.

The best thing is –The techniques used have been accumulated through many years of study and research and experience; this is no ordinary service! It is designed to show you approaches that will radically change your perspective, unlocking your potential to heal and create the shifts that will empower you to live a long and happy life.

I want you to know that I have been where you are now. I 'get it' and have used all of the techniques I will be using with you, in creating my future and tapping into the vast potential that is within every one of us to be healthy and happy and fulfil our destiny.

www.cancercoachuk.com

Contact Daniella at:

Web: www.cancercoachuk.com

Email: info@cancercoach-nlp.com

Phone: +44 (0)20 83193793
            +44 (0)7870 275257

Facebook: Cancer Coach

Twitter: Cancer Coach NLP

www.ingramcontent.com/pod-product-compliance
Lightning Source LLC
Chambersburg PA
CBHW072027040426
42447CB00009B/1764